WELSH

LEARN 35 WORDS TO SPEAK WELSH

Written by Peter Roberts and Geraint Davies

For the first-time visitor to Wales

An English/Welsh language book, teaching you how to speak Welsh using 35 selected useful words.

First edition: July 2016

Published in the United Kingdom
by
Russet Publishing
russetpublishing.com

Distributed internationally
by
Lulu Press Inc.
Raleigh, North Carolina, USA
lulu.com

Printed version
ISBN 978-1-910537-23-7

Not available as an electronic version

Copyright © 2016 Peter and Helena Roberts

Comments and corrections welcome to
peter.roberts@russetpublishing.com

"Learn 35 words" is the copyright trade phrase of Peter and Helena Roberts.

A WORD FROM THE AUTHORS

The Welsh in this book was written for us by our great friend Geraint Davies. He is a Welsh national, and taught English in Wales for a significant part of his career.

This piece of work, has been made for absolute beginners. We have received a good feedback from people using our 'Learn 35 words' system.

If you spot errors, please let us know. If you want to suggest corrections and improvements, or even just make general comments, please send them to us at:

peter.roberts@russetpublishing.com

Of course, if you have enjoyed our book, and if it helped you to enjoy your holiday, please also let us know. Many thanks.

Don't forget to learn the 35 words thoroughly *before* your holiday if you possibly can. On the other hand, perhaps it will wile away the time while you are there in a cafe in the rain, or under a sun umbrella on a hot beach, where you can order your glass of water or cup of coffee fluently in either venue.

Wherever you read it, we are sure that, when you have studied it, it will make all the difference. And remember that a language book will mean more to you and will help you to remember vocabulary if you write notes in it and add your own words and phrases!

Best wishes from Peter and Helena Roberts and Geraint Davies.

***Professional Input.** The core Welsh content of this booklet has been checked, corrected, and approved by a professional translation firm using a native-speaking Welsh translator.*

CONTENTS	5
INTRODUCTION	7
Chapter 1 LEARN THE 35 WORDS	9
Chapter 2 I WANT SOMETHING	17
Chapter 3 I WANT TO FIND SOMETHING	21
Chapter 4 I WANT TO BUY SOMETHING	25
Chapter 5 I WANTED TO SPEAK WELSH	29

INTRODUCTION

Learn 35 words. Speak Welsh

Yes, really! If you learn the 35 words that this book contains, you will be able to speak more Welsh than you ever thought possible in such a short time!

Try it and see. It will work! I did learn it when we wrote this book. Now I can speak quite good 'vacation' Welsh - Peter.

Yes, it will take some time to learn 35 words, but it will be worth it the minute you arrive in Wales and start to speak in Welsh! We'll show you how!

This book was prepared by us to help you get around more easily. We know that within only one week, you will be able to ask for things in restaurants and in the market. You will ask directions, buy tickets, get on a train and arrive at the required destination, and have a good time.

That's why we printed this small booklet - so that anyone who wants to have a holiday in Wales, and who doesn't know any Welsh, can 'have a go'. With confidence!

Chapter 1 of the book contains the list of 35 words that you will need to know, together with a phonetic guide to their pronunciation. You will find it easy to learn them - make sure you learn them with the correct pronunciation.

Remember, **pronunciation and emphasis are both very important**. Look at the phonetic part and practise each word <u>faster and faster</u> until it sounds like a single word. So that *uh-<u>ee</u>-shee-eye* becomes *uh-<u>ee</u>-shy*, which blends together to form the correct pronunciation of e<u>i</u>siau.

There is a general rule that we emphasise the <u>penultimate</u> syllable in a word, but in any event, we have marked any syllable requiring emphasis by underlining it.

When you have learned the list and tested yourself thoroughly, you can move on to Chapters 2, 3, and 4, which will show you how to use the 35 words so that you will be understood for most of what you will need on a Welsh holiday. And finally, we suggest a few nouns that you might find useful, by starting off your list of 'dictionary' words.

Why only 35 words?

Because then you won't have to struggle with a phrase book when you want to speak! No waiter, bus conductor, or Welsh citizen is going to hang about while you struggle in a book to find the phrase you want, is he?

We hope that you have a wonderful visit to Wales, and that upon your return, our little booklet encourages you to have lessons and *really* learn how to speak the language.

Peter and Geraint.

Chapter 1
Learn the 35 words.
Here's the magic list.

Unfortunately, there is no other way to learn this list but to sit down and study it for a few days. Our suggestion is that you set aside a regular time each day with someone else - preferably your proposed travel partner - and learn and test each other until you are absolutely sure that you know all of the words and can say their pronunciation correctly without thinking. Then you are ready to move on to Chapter 2.

The List

Don't forget that, in order to help you with the pronunciation, we have given a sort of amateur way of pronouncing each word, and we have underlined the part of the word that needs speaking strongly. i.e. emphasised. Practise until you can say each word quickly, and until you have remembered all of the words.

Hint: Learn words 3, 20, 22, 25, 32 and 35 first.

For pronunciation and gender guide, see pages 14 and 15, which you may wish to study first, before learning the list.

1	**a**		The indefinite article '**a**' does not exist in Welsh
2	**also**		hefyd
		pronounced:	<u>heh</u>-vid
3	**and**		a *before a consonant* ac *before a vowel*
		pronounced:	ah *and* ak *respectively*
4	**the bill**		y <u>bil</u>
		pronounced:	uh <u>bill</u> (as in the English)
5	**but**		ond
		pronounced:	ond
6	**cold**		<u>o</u>er
		pronounced:	<u>oh</u>-eer
7	**do you have…?**		oes <u>genn</u>ych chi…?
		pronounced:	oys <u>gen</u>-nikh kee
8	**excuse me**		esgus<u>o</u>dwch fi
		pronounced:	es-guss-<u>od</u>-ookh vee
9	**exit (out; outside)**		all<u>a</u>nfa (<u>all</u>an)
		pronounced:	ath-<u>lan</u>-va ('th' as in think)
10	**free of charge**		heb <u>dâl</u>
		pronounced:	heb <u>daal</u>

11	**a glass**		glasiad
		pronounced:	gla-shiad
12	**good**		da (masculine)
			dda (feminine) where dda is
		pronounced:	thaa (th as in 'that')
13	**good evening**		noswaith dda
		pronounced:	noss-wa-eeth thaa
14	**good morning**		bore da
		pronounced:	bor-eh da
15	**hot** (or spicy)		poeth
		pronounced:	po-ith (th as in 'thin')
16	**how much** (is it)?		faint?
		pronounced:	va-eent *becomes* vine-t
17	**is** (same as **'are'**)		mae
		pronounced:	ma-ee (my)
	is there a		oes y na?
		pronounced:	oys na
18	**no**		na! no tea
		pronounced:	nah! dim te (dim teh)
19	**of**		o
		pronounced:	o (as in office)

20	**one** (1)		un
		pronounced:	een (actually, French une)

21	**or**		n<u>e</u>u
		pronounced:	<u>nuh</u>-yee

22	**please**		os gwelwch yn <u>dd</u>a
		pronounced:	oss-gwel-ookh un <u>thaa</u>

23	**small**		b<u>y</u>chan
		pronounced:	bu<u>kh</u>-an

24	**station**		<u>g</u>orsaf
		pronounced:	<u>g</u>orr-sav
			police station: <u>g</u>orsaf <u>hedd</u>lu
			train station: gorsaf tren,
			bus station: gorsaf bws

25	**thank you**		d<u>i</u>olch
		pronounced:	<u>dee</u>-olkh

26	**that one**		hwna
		pronounced:	<u>hoo</u>-na

27	**the**		y
		pronounced:	uh before a consonant
		pronounced:	ur before a vowel
			e.g. uh <u>g</u>orsav, ur ath-<u>lan</u>-va
			the station the exit

28	**this** (this one)	hwn
	pronounced:	hoon (as in English 'foot')
29	**ticket**	to<u>c</u>yn
	pronounced:	<u>tok</u>-in
30	**the toilets** (public)	y toil<u>ed</u>au
	pronounced:	uh toy-<u>led</u>-eye
31	**train**	trên
	pronounced:	train (as in English train)
		trên i Bangor ('i' as 'ee')
		the train to Bangor
		'i' above is pronounced 'ee'
32	**two** (2)	<u>d</u>au
	pronounced:	<u>da</u>-ee (die)
33	**I want (would like)**	rydw i e<u>is</u>iau (polite)
	pronounced:	rrudd-oo ee u-<u>ee</u>-shy
	I do not want	rydw i <u>dim</u> e<u>is</u>iau
	pronounced:	rrudd-oo ee <u>dim</u> uh-<u>ee</u>-shy
34	**where?** (Where is?)	lle? (lle m<u>ae</u>?)
	pronounced:	thlay <u>ma</u>-ee (thlay my)
		(th as in the English think)
35	**yes**	<u>i</u>a
	pronounced:	<u>ee</u>-ah

To help with your pronunciation:

ch is pronounced as in the Scottish word loch, which we have written as kh in phonetic parts.

ll is pronounced 'thl' as in no English word but attempt 'thl'. i.e. 'Llanelly' is pronounced 'Thlanethly' and 'allan' is pronounced 'athlan'.

u is pronounced 'i' is in pin and that is as near as most English speakers will get.

f is pronounced v as in the English word 'velvet'.

ff is pronounced f as in the English word 'fist'.

dd is pronounced th, as in the English word 'this'.

th is pronounced as in the English word 'thing'.

w is pronounced as the u in the English word 'foot' (not as in the English word 'hoot'.

i is pronounced ee as in the English word 'heel', with exceptions 'dim' and 'bil'.

e is pronounced ay as in the English word 'pay'.

y is pronounced i as in 'pin' if it is in the last syllable of a multi - syllable word, and whenever it follows a letter w. Elsewhere (including single syllable words) it is pronounced uh as in the English word 'cup'.

r. <u>Always</u> enunciate the letter r in words, <u>even at the end of a word</u> - especially at the end of a word. In English it is silent after a vowel, but in Welsh it is spoken and even rolled - indicated in this book as rr.

In Welsh, nouns can be either masculine or feminine, but we just use the same word 'y' for the word 'the', irrespective of gender.

Also there are many complicated rules of mutation, where words change their form in Welsh, and yet we have been obliged not to implement them in this book owing to its very basic nature.

Please note that in Welsh, the adjective follows the noun, so that 'small glass' becomes *'glass small'* - <u>gl</u>asiad <u>by</u><u>ch</u>an.

- - - - - - - - oOo - - - - - - - -

So, have you really learned the magic 35 words? Or perhaps not!

If you have not, then go back to the list and keep learning until you can recall the words with no difficulty.

As we said before, learning the list is the hardest part of this job, but it won't take long if you really work at it. The morning time is the best time to learn things - when you are fresh. It's hard work in the evening when you're tired. So, find the first morning that you can - preferably before you go on holiday - and start to learn the list of 35 words. Then relearn them the day after, and the day after and the day after. Five half hour sessions over five days will be much better than one two-and-a-half hour session. Of course, it's even possible to learn the words while you're on holiday. At least you'll have some time to do it.

If possible, ask a friend to test you, until you are perfect.

Normally, to speak Welsh, you will need about three years of hard effort and a private tutor. Most people don't want to put in that kind of effort or expense. For a first holiday to a different country, it's not necessary either. We know, because we've tried it.

On the other hand, it's frustrating on a holiday if you can't speak anything at all, and you feel you'd like to try to say something in Welsh in a café, at a station, in the city, or when you want to buy something at a countryside stall or in a village shop. So, the following chapters show you how to put 35 words together to speak Welsh! It's true!

Now that you have learned the magic 35 words, it will take you next to no time to learn how to string them together to say lots of useful things. You will be speaking Welsh in no time at all.

OK! Now we'll show you how to put the words together to speak Welsh!

Chapter 2
I want something.
Don't we all?

Yes we all want something - mostly all of the time. We need a drink of water - especially in the summer in Wales.

We need to ask for lots of things like drinks, food, tickets in stations, the bill in a café, and so on.

OK. Believe it or not you already know how to do this!

I want….. It's a very useful statement, but it sounds a bit brusque in English, so we exchange it for the phrase 'I would like to have". That's better! And in Welsh, we have to use the three words *'Rydw i eisiau'*. You want something and it says it politely.

Rydw i eisiau. I want.   That's it - it's in the list of 35 words.

What do you want? Lots of things, especially a drink of tea or coffee. You already know the word for tea - we didn't have to put it on our list. It's *te* (pronounced *teh*).

Or, rather than saying that you actually want something, you can say, in a less direct way, while you consider things:

oes gennych chi…? which simply asks, "Do you have…?

or, even more briefly, you can just ask 'oys na…?' which means 'are there…?' or 'is there…?'

Do you have tea?   Oes gennich chi te?
Is there tea?   Oys na teh?
Is there an apple?   Oys na aval? *(ah-val)*
Are there apples?   Oys na afalau? *(Oys na a-val-eye)*
Is there decaf coffee? Oys na coffi heb caffein?
                                    (heb kaff-een)

Tea please.   *Te, os gwelwch yn dda.*
Or, more fully: *Rydw i eisiau te, os gwelwch yn dda.*
Green tea   *Te gwyrdd* pronounced (gwi-rr-th)
             (dd pronounced - 'th' as in 'the'.)
                where *gwyrdd* is the Welsh for 'green'.

You can specify green tea by saying:
Rydw i eisiau te gwyrdd, os gwelwch yn dda.
te gwyrdd (teh gwi-rr-th) wi as in 'wig', th as in 'that'.

You can also specify the teabag out of the water by saying, "Please put the teabag outside the tea pot."
Os gwelwch yn dda, rhowch y bag te tu allan i'r pot te.
(*rrowch* is thro-ookh, and *tu* is pronounced tee. (tee athlan meaning outside) (th as in think). If you can pronounce French perfectly, then the Welsh word 'tu' is pronounced exactly like the French word for you - 'tu', but 'tee' is the nearest most English-speaking people will get to it.)

18

That's it, and it says it all doesn't it? You can already order some tea in a cafe. And they will understand what you want. You'll get your tea the way you like it.

There is also coffee (<u>c</u>offi), pronounced *<u>ko</u>-fee*.
If you want black coffee, the Welsh say 'coffe black' ...
<u>co</u>ffi du. (pronounced *dee*)
and for white coffee, they say 'coffee white' ...
<u>co</u>ffi gwyn. (pronounced *goo-in*) oo as in 'foot'.

Rydw i e<u>is</u>iau un <u>c</u>offi du. (een <u>ko</u>-fee dee)
I want one black coffee.

with sugar   g<u>y</u>da siwgr *(pronounced <u>guh</u>-da shugar)*
with milk   g<u>y</u>da <u>ll</u>aeth (guh-da <u>thly</u>-th) th as in 'think'.
without caffeine   heb <u>c</u>affein (heb <u>ka</u>-feen) <u>c</u>offi heb <u>ka</u>-feen

And to top it off and make it sound even more polite, we add the words for 'please' - os gwelwch yn <u>dda</u>.

Rydw i e<u>is</u>iau un <u>c</u>offi du, os gwelwch yn <u>dda</u>.
I want one black coffee, please.

Rydw i e<u>is</u>iau coffi gwyn, os gwelwch yn <u>dda</u>.
I would like a white coffee, please.

Rydw i e<u>is</u>iau <u>g</u>lasiad o dŵr, os gwelwch yn <u>dda</u>.
I want a glass of water please.

Mae hwn yn dda pronounced ma-ee hoon un thaa.
This is good.   (oo as in 'foot')

Rydw i eisiau potel o dŵr gyda gas, os gwelwch yn dda.
I want a bottle of sparkling water please.
potel (pronounced pot-ell) means 'bottle' or 'a bottle'.
dŵr (doo-er) means water.
gyda gas. (guh-da means 'with').

If you don't want your water fizzy, that's easy too. You don't have to try to think up an equivalent phrase for the English words 'still water', you just say "heb gas", which means 'without gas'.

Rydw i eisiau dau lemonêd, os gwelwch yn dda
I want two lemonades, please.

Rydw i eisiau y bil, os gwelwch yn dda.
I want the bill please - in the restaurant or bar. Perhaps you actually don't, in which case you can tell your friends:
Rydw i dim eisiau y bil, diolch.   *(bil pronounced 'bill')*
I don't want the bill, thank you.

That's it - you are in control of the situation in the cafe. And you always added 'please' - *os gwelwch yn dda* and 'thank you' - di*olch*. By the way, did you pay the bill after all?

20

Chapter 3
To find something.
We often need to find places.

We all need to find something - mostly all of the time.

We need to know where to get a train, or a taxi, or where to buy a paper or a stamp. We need to find the right train. We need to find a garage. We need to ask for lots of things.

Most commonly, in our experience, we need to find the ladies or gents toilets.

No problem. You already know how to do this from your list of 35 words. You did say you'd learned them didn't you?

Lle mae - 'where is' or 'where are'.
Pronounced: thlay ma-ee (or thlay my).

It's pretty easy.

lle mae'r gwesty?	Where is the hotel?
(goo-est-ee or gwesty)	
Lle mae tacsi?	Where is a taxi?

Or you could try a phrase we use very often, which asks if there is a certain thing nearby.
Use ger<u>llaw</u> (ger-<u>thla</u>-oo), meaning 'nearby'.

Oys na t<u>a</u>csi ger<u>llaw</u>?
is there a taxi nearby?

Oys na fferyllfa gerllaw?
Oys na fer-uh-thl-va ger-<u>thla</u>-oo?
is there a pharmacy nearby?

Lle m<u>ae</u>'r toi<u>led</u>au? (toy-<u>led</u>-eye) Where are the toilets?
Lle m<u>ae</u>'r t<u>oi</u>led?   Where is the toilet?

Lle mae'r toi<u>led</u>au, os gwelwch yn <u>dd</u>a?
Where are the toilets, please?

It's not worth learning the words for male and female because 99% of toilet doors in public places have a symbol of a man or a woman on them - standard all over the world. You'll see which door is right for you when you get there!

Lle mae'r <u>g</u>orsaf <u>bws</u>?   <u>g</u>orsaf <u>trên</u>
Where is the bus station?   *train station*

Lle mae <u>banc</u>?
Where is a bank?

Lle mae'r Hilton Hotel?
Where is the Hilton Hotel?

Of course, we can add 'please' to make it more polite.

Lle mae'r Hilton Hotel, os gwelwch yn dda?
Where is the Hilton Hotel, please?

Lle mae'r mynedfa? pronounced: mun-ed-va
Where is the entrance?
Lle mae'r allanfa? pronounced: ath-lan-va
Where is the exit?

Anyone who speaks fluent Welsh will tell you that the above sentences are basic. But they will work! That's the main thing. They are not grammatically perfect, but they will allow you to be understood.

In Wales, you could, of course, simply speak English, since everyone understands and speaks it, but that's not what you are trying to achieve, is it? You are trying to show respect to the Welsh people, and have some enjoyment at the same time, by speaking a few words of the Welsh language. That's why you bought this book, after all.

ADD YOUR OWN NOTES AND NEW WORDS HERE:

Chapter 4
To buy something.
Don't we all want to do that?

Yes we all want to buy something during our holidays - mostly all of the time. We need to buy presents, food, tickets, papers, postcards, etcetera.

So we could try to teach you a list of a hundred different things that you might want to buy. However, to save you the trouble most of the time, you can learn two words that will stand in for nearly everything: 'this', and 'that'.

Nonetheless, if you're smart, you'll buy a small, English/Welsh/English pocket dictionary from your local bookshop before you visit Wales. Then you'll have a list of thousands of things that you can ask for.

Ultimately, of course, you can use your finger to point to something when you want it.

I want this! or I want that! It's easy in English - and in Welsh

You learned the words on the list so…

Rydw i ei__siau hwn. (I would like this) or *Rydw i ei__siau hwna, os gwelwch yn dda. (I would like that, please).*

It's easy. Now you can ask for anything in the world that you can actually see at the time. I want to buy this or I want to buy that. Just point to it. What could be easier?

If you want to look up words, then that is also fine. For example, you might want to look up the word for a postcard, or a stamp, and then ask for them in the shop, because you might not be able to see a stamp to point to.

If you look up the word for stamp in a dictionary, you will find that it's called a '*stamp*', just the same as in English!

So you walk up to the counter in the shop/post office and say: *Rydw i ei__siau un stamp - i Amer__ica, os gwelwch yn dda.* It is simple but they will understand you! "I want one stamp - to America". You are polite using '*os gwelwch yn dda*'.

Before you buy something, you may wish to check how much it would cost. So you need the word *'faint'* from the list of 35 words that you learned. Just use it followed by 'please' to simply say 'How much, please?' Meaning *'how much does it cost, please?'* Brief, but polite.

Or to be a bit more adventurous, you could say:
Faint yw hwn? How much is this?
(pronounced *va-eent ee-oo hoon*)

Or when you have bought something, you could say:
Faint yw hwna? How much is that?
(pronounced *va-eent ee-oo hoona,* with oo as in 'foot')

In Wales, some people may use English numbers, but most people will use Welsh, so if you intend to stay in Wales for a while or go there occasionally, you may find it worthwhile learning Welsh numbers.

But, of course, everyone speaks English - especially if you ask. And, in any case, you can often see on the electronic till how much the thing is if you are buying it, so that's fairly easy!

If people were to reply to you in Welsh, you wouldn't know enough to understand the number they say back to you - which would be a problem - and which is why we have not intruduced words such as 'why?', 'how', or 'what?'.

In the case of difficulty, just ask someone to please speak in English.

ADD YOUR OWN NOTES AND NEW WORDS HERE:

We are starting off a list of new words that you might have looked up in a small dictionary. Please continue adding some more as you go along.

police - heddlu *(heth-lee)*   then - yna *(uh-na)*

if - os *(oss)*

doctor - meddyg *(meth-ig)*   *pronounce* 'th' is as in 'this'

hospital - ysbyty *(uss-but-ee)*

postcard - cerdyn post *(ker-din poste)*

café - caffi   *(ka-fee)*

restaurant - bwyty *(boo-witty)*

....

....

....

....

....

....

Chapter 5
To speak Welsh.
Your dream.

You wanted to speak Welsh when you bought this book.

Well now you can. With just the 35 words we have taught you, you can speak an awful lot.

You won't believe it until you try, but you can get by for an entire holiday. And, if you have bought a small dictionary, you will learn another 35 words while you are away and you will be well on your way. You might even go to classes back home and improve more. Who knows?

Anyway, here are some of the things that you can now say that you never thought you would.

Rydw i ei<u>s</u>iau un coffi ma<u>wr</u> heb <u>c</u>aff<u>e</u>in.
I want one large decaffeinated coffee.
mawr (pronounced ma-<u>oor</u>) means large or big.

Rydw i ei<u>s</u>iau dau te.   (da-ee teh becomes die teh)
I want two teas.

Lle <u>ma</u>e'r <u>g</u>orsaf tren, os gwelwch yn <u>dd</u>a?
Where is the railway station, please?

Lle mae'r tren i Caerdydd? (Ka-ir-dith. 'th' as in 'the')
Where is the train to Cardiff?

Faint yw hwn? Y cerdyn post?
(Va-eent ee-oo hoon? Uh ker-din poste?)
How much is this? The postcard?

Rydw i ei<u>si</u>au y bil, os gwelwch yn <u>dda</u>.
I want the bill, please.

Rydw i eisiau un coffi mawr a dau glasiad o lemonêd, os gwelwch yn dda.
I want one coffee and two glasses of lemonade, please.

Esgu<u>so</u>dwch fi. Lle mae'r Ritz hotel, os gwelwch yn dda?
Excuse me. Where is the Ritz hotel, please?

You get on a bus and ask the driver or passengers 'Esgusodwch fi, i Caerdydd?' (*Excuse me. For Cardiff?*) Simple. They will either nod and mutter 'ia' or say 'na' and point you in the right direction. This should get you there.

Lle mae ta<u>c</u>si, os gwelwch yn dda?
Where is a taxi, please?

Rydw i eisiau cwrw, os gwelwch yn dda. (koo-roo)
I want a beer, please.

Red wine (*gwin coch*), pronounced *gween caukh*, where gwin means wine, and coch means red.

Or white wine (*gwin gwyn*), pronounced *gween gwin*.
Rydw i ei̱siau gla̱siad o gwin gwyn, os gwelwch yn d̲d̲a.
I want a glass of white wine, please.

Rydw i eisiau po̱tel o gwin gwyn, os gwelwch yn d̲d̲a.
I want a bottle of white wine please.

Don't you think that this is great? You have learned 35 words (plus a few more sneakily) and you are speaking Welsh on your holiday. Well done!

And there are some lined and blank pages throughout this booklet where you can add your own new words. Soon you'll know a lot more than the 35 core words in the list. In fact, we have already offered you another 35 words in the sections on how to use the language. Just keep going!

Please remember that what you have learned here is very basic and is just a start. To speak Welsh well, you need to read proper textbooks and go to classes with a good teacher. Or even get private lessons. We hope we have given you the incentive to do so.

But if you don't study the language more deeply, you can always take our booklet with you when you go to Wales again!

With best wishes,

Peter and Geraint.

Printed in Great
Britain
by Amazon